F…

Quintus, a y… stationed in … times, falls in lo… can't marry be… and he must win … on a three-year camp… …ia to subdue the Painted … in the wilds of Caledonia. The story of how Quintus is made Centurion brings vividly to life the stirring times when Rome conquered the known world, and make exciting reading for the under-eights.

Rosemary Sutcliff is the author of such novels as *The Eagle of the Ninth*, *The Silver Branch*, *The Lantern Bearers* and most recently *Frontier Wolf*, which are all set in Roman Britain, and few writers of historical fiction have her ability to bring to life far-off times so vividly. *A Circlet of Oak Leaves*, also written for younger readers, is available in Beavers.

Eagle's Egg

Rosemary Sutcliff

Illustrated by Victor Ambrus

Beaver Books

First published in 1981 by
Hamish Hamilton Children's Books Limited
Garden House, 57–59 Long Acre, London WC2E 9J2

This paperback edition published in 1982 by
The Hamlyn Publishing Group Limited
London · New York · Sydney · Toronto
Astronaut House, Feltham, Middlesex, England

ISBN 0 600 2047 5

Reproduced, printed and bound in Great Britain by
Hazell Watson & Viney Ltd, Aylesbury, Bucks
Set in Baskerville

Contents

1 The Girl at the Well *7*

2 Marching Orders *20*

3 Campaign in the North *31*

4 Eagle's Egg *36*

5 The Last Battle *53*

6 Return to Eburacum *69*

1

The Girl at the Well

All right then, if it's a story you're wanting, throw another log on the fire. The winters strike colder now than they used to do when I was a young man in Britain: and I'll tell you. . . .

Eburacum was a frontier station in my father's day; your great-grandfather's. But Roman rule spread northward in one way and another; and by the time I was posted up there as Eagle Bearer to the Ninth Legion it wasn't a frontier station any more, and the settlement that had gathered itself together under the fortress walls had become a sizeable town, with a forum where the business of the place was carried on, and wine shops, and temples to half a score of different gods.

Well, so I was ambling up the narrow, crooked street behind the temple of Sulis on one of those dark edge-of-spring evenings when it seems as though all the colour has drained out of the world and left only the grey behind. I was off duty and I was bored. I'd been down to the lower end of the town to look at some new young fighting cocks that Kaeso had for sale, but I hadn't liked the look of any that he had shown me, and taking it all in all, I was feeling thoroughly out at elbows with the world. And then I rounded the corner of the temple garden; and there, at the well that bubbled up from under the wall, a few paces further up the street, a girl was drawing water. And I knew I'd been wrong about there being no colour left in the world, because her hair lit up that grey street like a dandelion growing on a stubble pile.–No, that's not right either, it was redder and more sparkling; a colour that you could warm your hands at. And the braids of it, hanging forward over her shoulders 'thick as a swordsman's wrist' as the saying goes.

You can guess the next bit, I dare say. Up I strolled, and stood beside her, and gave her my best smile when she turned round.

'That pail is much too heavy for a little bird like you,' said I. 'Better let me carry it for you.'

She stood and looked at me out of the bluest and brightest eyes I'd ever seen in any girl's head; not smiling back, but as though something amused her, all the same: and I got the feeling that I was not the first of our lads who had offered to carry her bucket home for her from the well of Sulis.

'It is not, really,' she said, 'and I am quite used to it.'

' "Never carry your own bucket if you can find somebody else to carry it for you". That's what we say in the Legions, more or less,' I told her. And I picked up the brimming pail from where she had set it on the well curb, and stood ready to carry it wherever she wanted.

'Then – that is our house, yonder at the bend of the street,' she said. 'The one with the workshop beside it and the big blue flower painted on the wall.'

And the laughter was still in her, because I had hoped it was much further off than that; and she knew it.

I should have to make the most of the

little distance there was. I walked as slowly as possible, making a great show of not spilling the water, and said, 'Why have I not seen you before? With that bonny brightness of hair I couldn't have missed you.'

'I do have a cloak with a hood to it,' she said. And then, stopping her teasing. 'But indeed I have not been long in Eburacum. My brother is making the picture-floor in the new Council Chamber, and he brought me up with him from Lindum, because he thinks that a growing town like this would be a good place for a craftsman to settle.'

And then we had reached the door, and I put the pail down, and she thanked me. We stood for an instant looking at each other, and an odd thing happened. We both turned shy.

'Do you go to the well at the same time every day?' I managed at last.

And she said, 'Most days, yes,' already picking up the bucket.

'Maybe we'll meet there again, some time—' I began. But before I could finish, she had gone in, and the door was quietly and gently shut in my face.

I did not even know her name.

Well, I could probably get that from her brother if I went along to the Council Chamber and admired his floor. I had seen and spoken with him more than once already. No problem there. But the girl had not really gone deep with me, yet, and I strolled back to the fortress thinking about the Council House and the things that had led up to it.

It was just about a year since the General Agricola had come out from Rome with orders to bring Caledonia, away north of us, within the frontiers of the Empire. He had taken the Second and Fourteenth Legions and pushed up through South Western Caledonia, and pegged down the country with a handful of forts and marching camps. – A friend of mine who was with the Second at the time told me it was pretty dull: not much serious fighting because the local tribes didn't know how to combine and seemingly hadn't found a leader strong enough to hammer them into one war-host.

At summer's end, when Agricola came back out of the wilds, he let it be known that there would be help from the Treasury for any town that liked to smarten itself up, with a new bath-house, say, or a council chamber or a triumphal arch. Somehow he'd got it into the heads of the local chiefs that it was beneath their dignity to live in towns that looked like broken-down rookeries, while in the south of Britain the people had public buildings that Rome herself would not be ashamed of. So architects and craftsmen were got up from the south and back in the autumn Eburacum had started building a fine new Council Chamber.

It had been a mild winter, and so the work had gone forward most of the time, and by winter's end most of the work was done and the thick fluted roof tiles were in place, so that the floor could be begun. A real Roman picture-floor that was to be the chief glory of the place. In the early days the Elders had meant to bring in a Roman artist. But after a while, when the money began to run short, they had had to shorten their ideas to match.

And so came Vedrix, up from Lindum, instead. I've always been interested in seeing how things are made; and so, as I

say, I'd already got into the way of wandering along sometimes, when I was off-duty, to watch him at work with his hammer and chisel, cutting his little cubes of chalk and sandstone, and brick and blue shale, and fitting them together into his picture.

A fiery little runt of a man, he was, with a white bony face that changed all the time, and hair like a bunch of carrots – and that's an odd thing, too, because later, when I saw him and his sister together, their hair was the same colour; and yet hers never made me think of a bunch of carrots – and a lame leg that he told me once had mended short after he broke it when he was a boy. But he was the kind of artist-craftsman who could turn his hand to most things and make a good job of them. So later on, when that floor was finished, it was a pretty good floor on the whole, though I still think the leopard looked a bit odd. But I suppose when you remember that he had never seen a real one, and had only a painted leopard on a cracked wine jar to copy, the wonder is that it didn't look odder still

But, I'm getting ahead of myself. The

picture-floor was only just a few days begun when I first saw my red-haired girl at the Well of Sulis. I spent a good deal of my free time watching it grow in the next few days also, for if I'd found Vedrix an interesting fellow to talk to before I knew he was brother to the bonniest girl in all Eburacum, I certainly didn't find him less interesting afterwards.

2

Marching Orders

I didn't ask him her name, though. Somehow I found I didn't want to ask that of anyone but herself. So I waited, and for quite a while I was not off duty at the right time again. But at last the waiting was over, and we both chanced together once more at the Well of Sulis; and I carried her pail home for her again; and that time we got as far as telling each other our names on the door-sill.

'Now that we've met again, we should know each other's names,' I said. 'Mine is Quintus, what is yours?'

'Cordaella,' she said, tucking in the ends of her hair that were being teased out by the wind.

'That's a beautiful name,' said I. 'It fits you.'

And suddenly she laughed at me. 'So I have been told.' And she ran inside and shut the door on me again.

Then the day came when I had the sneezing fever.

'Do they not give you anything for that, up at the fort?' she said.

I had a sudden picture inside my head, of myself going up on Sick Parade, to bother Manlius the fort surgeon with my snufflings, and what he would say if I did. And that made me laugh so much despite my aching head, that I started coughing again, and leant against the doorpost choking and sneezing enough to put any girl off me for life. But she turned suddenly kind, and said, 'Come you in to the fire, and I will give you something. I have some herb skill, even if your fat fort surgeon has none.'

And she brought me in and sat me down by the fire on the central hearth of the warm smoky house-place; and she set the old slave-woman who came out of the shadows at her call, to heating water in a little bronze pot over the flames, while she herself fetched herbs and a lump of honeycomb from some inner place; and when they had boiled all up together, she poured the brew off into a cup and gave it to me, saying, 'Now, drink – as hot as you can.'

So, more to please her than for any faith I had in it, I sipped and snuffled my way through the scalding brew. It was sweet with the honey and greasy with the melted comb-wax, and the smoke of all the nameless herbs that had gone into it seemed to go right to the back of my nose and drift around inside my skull, so that for a moment I thought the top was coming off my head. But in a little it began to ease the aching, and truly I think that I began to mend from that moment.

Aye well, in one way and another, we contrived to see quite a bit of each other as that spring drew on. And after a while I kissed her, and she kissed me back as sweet as a hazel-nut. But it was after we had kissed each other, that we began to be unhappy. More and more unhappy. I daresay that sounds odd and the wrong way round, but we had our

reasons, – seeing that the Legions don't allow any marrying 'below the vine staff'; below the rank of Centurion, that is.

'Maybe you will get promotion,' Cordaella said again and again.

But I wasn't very hopeful. It seemed to me that what I wanted was so tremendous that the gods would surely never give it to me. 'Maybe,' I said, 'and maybe not. Anyway it will not be for a long time, and your brother has other plans for you. You told me so yourself.'

'There are two words as to my brother's plans,' said Cordaella, with a sniff. But there could be no sniffing at the Legion's rule about marrying below the vine staff.

I went round by the new Council Chamber on my way back to barracks, to have a word with Vedrix. I hadn't much idea what I was going to say to him, but there might be something; and anyway it was better than not saying or doing anything at all.

I heard the light tapping of his little hammer before I came in from the forecourt, and there he was squatting among his sticks of shale and sandstone, cutting them up into fine pavement cubes and setting them in place in the pattern. He was working on the ivy-leaf border, and I did not interrupt him; just stood looking, until he came to a good stopping place and sat back on his heels and grinned up at me like a fox.

'Odd to think of our Elders sitting here solemnly in their Roman tunics and on carved Roman chairs, to settle the affairs of the city. Not so long ago, when there was any settling to be done, the chiefs gathered to the council fire, and sat on their spread bulls'-hides with their weapons left outside.'

'Ever so civilised it's getting in these parts,' I said.

He shrugged. 'So the noble General Agricola would have us believe. If we are busy enough being Roman and civilised, we shall not notice that we are only strengthening our own bondage.'

There was a sudden harsh silence, and then I heard my own voice saying, 'You mind, don't you? I did not think that you minded.'

'Because I make a picture-pavement

for the Romans and the British-Romans?' he said; and then, carefully fitting another cube into its place, 'How should I not mind that Rome rules me and my people, who have been free?'

'I don't know,' I floundered a bit. 'I suppose I thought – well, artists and poets and such don't seem to mind so much about who actually holds the rule, so long as they can get on with making their statutes or their songs as they like.'

Vedrix set another little cube in place, settling it down with his round-nosed mallet. 'We of the Tribes,' he said, 'we don't divide people up, as you Romans do, into neat bundles – soldiers or tent-makers or wine merchants or poets. I'd have been out with the fighting men in the Troubles three years since, but for this short leg of mine. – I can handle a spear as well as most, but I'm slow on the hills, and that makes a man dangerous to his comrades.'

'I'm sorry,' I said awkwardly.

He turned a cube of blue shale over in his fingers, and bent to settle it in place. 'You have no need to be,' he said, very carefully.

'No,' I stumbled, 'not about that. – I'm sorry I got it wrong about tent-makers and poets.' I felt the whole conversation getting away from me, and certainly getting further every moment from what I had come to talk to him about. I took a deep breath, and swallowed, 'Vedrix,' I said, 'I want to talk to you seriously about something, and you're making it all more and more difficult.'

'So? I am listening. Speak then, as seriously as you please.'

Somehow, almost without knowing it, I slipped into the British tongue, the Celtic tongue. I had grown used to speaking it, after a fashion, with Cordaella, for the Celtic is better than the Latin, for making love-talk to a British girl, and easier for explaining to her brother in, too.

I said, 'The love is upon me, for Cordaella.'

He abandoned the pavement and looked up at me, and answered in his own tongue also. 'And is the love upon Cordaella for you?'

'Yes,' I said.

'You sound very sure, my fine young Roman Standard-bearer.'

'I am,' I said. 'She told me.'

'And did she tell you that I have already found for her a man of her own people before we left Lindum?'

'Yes, with thirty head of cattle.'

'You, I am thinking, do not have thirty head of cattle. And yet you would be marrying with the girl in his stead.'

'I would!' I said, 'But I cannot – not yet anyway.'

'And why would that be?' said he, with his red brows quirking up towards the roots of his hair.

'In the Legions, no one below the rank of Centurion—'

'Is allowed to take a wife, ah yes. And so you will be needing promotion before she grows weary of waiting. Well – good luck to you, noble Standard-bearer.'

Suddenly I began to feel a flicker of hope.

'You mean – you'll not force her to go to this other man?'

'Force Cordaella?' he said. 'In all the years since our father died, I have never found the way to make Cordaella do anything she was set against. If ever you do marry her, it may be that you will find the way, but I very much doubt it. Far more likely it will be the other way round!'

'I'll risk it,' I said; and all at once it was as though the sun came out.

And then the trumpet sounded from the fort, and I knew that I must be getting back.

3

Campaign in the North

Later the same day I was standing before the piled writing-table in the Headquarters Office, where Dexius Valens the Senior Centurion had sent for me, waiting for him to notice that I was there. After a while he looked up from the scatter of tablets and papyrus rolls before him, and said, 'Ah, Standard-bearer. – Yes, the General Agricola is at Corstopitum overseeing the arrangements for this summer's Caledonian Campaign. The order has just come through. – We march to join him in three days.'

So that was that. All town leave was stopped, of course, and I never even got to see Cordaella to say farewell to her. Couldn't write her a note, either, because of course she couldn't read anyway. The best I could do was to scratch a few lines to Vedrix and ask him to read them to her

– I thought I could trust him – and get one of the mule-drivers to take the letter down into the town the next day.

And three days later, leaving the usual holding-garrison behind us, we marched out for Corstopitum.

A Legion on the march – that's something worth the seeing; the long winding column, cohort after cohort, the cavalry wings spread on either side and the baggage train following after. A great serpent of mailed men, red-hackled with the crests of the officers' helmets, and whistling whatever tune best pleases them at the moment – 'Payday' perhaps, or 'The Emperor's Wineskins', or 'The Girl I kissed at Clusium', to keep the marching time. Four miles to the hour, never slower, never faster, uphill and down, twenty miles a day. . . . And me, marching up at the head, right behind the Legate on his white horse, carrying the great Eagle of the Legion, with the sunlight splintering on its spread wings; and its talons clutched on the lighting-jags of Jupiter, and the gilded laurel wreaths of its victories. . . .

Aye, I was the proud one, that day! For

I'd seen Cordaella among the crowd that gathered to see us off, and she had seen me and waved to me. And I was through with garrison duty and going to join the fighting, and win my promotion and maybe make a name for myself and come back with the honours shining on my breast; and all for my girl Cordaella. And my breast swelled as though the honours were already there. – What a bairn I was, what a boy with my head chock-full of dreams of glory, for all the great lion-skin that I wore over my armour, and the size of my hands on the Eagle shaft, and my long legs eating up the Northward miles!

But it was three years and more before we came marching back; and there were times when I came near to forgetting Cordaella for a while, though never quite.

4

Eagle's Egg

We joined Agricola with the Twentieth Legion at Corstopitum, and marched on North across the great Lowland hills until we were joined by the main part of the Second and the Fourteenth that had come up through the western country of last summer's campaigning. Then we headed on for the broad Firth that all but cuts Caledonia in half. The Fleet met us there, and we spent the rest of the summer making a naval base. You need something of that sort for supplies, and support, when you can't be sure of your land lines of communication behind you. We saw a bit of fighting from time to time, but seemingly the Lowland chiefs were still too busy fighting with each other, to make a strong show against us, so mostly it was just building; first the supply base, and then with the winter

scarce past, a string of turf and timber forts right across the low-lying narrows of the land.

Sick and tired we got of it, too, and there began to be a good deal of grumbling. I mind Lucius, a mate of mine growling into his supper bannock that he might as well have stayed at home and been a builder's labourer – and me trying to give him the wink that the Cohort Commander was standing right behind him. It's odd, the small daft things not worth remembering, that one remembers across half a lifetime. . . .

But in the next spring, when we started the big push on into the Highlands, we found a difference.

Somehow, sometime in that second winter, the Caledonians had found the leader they needed to hammer them into one people. Calgacus, his name was, I never saw him, not until the last battle; but I got so that the bare mention of his name would have me looking over my shoulder and reaching for my sword. It was the same with all of us, especially when the mists came down from the high tops or rain blotted out the bleak

country as far as a man could see. Oh yes, we saw plenty enough fighting that summer, to make up for any breathing space we'd had in the two before.

Agricola was too cunning a fox to go thrusting his muzzle up into the mountains, with every turf of bog-cotton seemingly a war-painted warrior in disguise, waiting to close the glens like a trap on his tail. Instead, he closed them himself, with great forts in the mouths of each one where it came down to the eastern plain. That way, there was no risk of the tribes swarming down unchecked to take us in the rear or cut our supply lines after we had passed by.

We got sullen-sick of fort building, all over again, yes; especially with our shoulder-blades always on the twitch for an arrow between them. The Ninth wintered at Inchtuthil, the biggest of the forts. The place was not finished, but we sat in the middle and went on building it round us, which is never a very comfortable state of things, in enemy country. We lost a lot of men in one way and another; and the old ugly talk of the Ninth being an unlucky Legion woke up

and began to drift round again. It might have been better if the Legate had not had a convenient bout of stomach trouble and gone south to winter in Corstopitum. I didn't envy Senior Centurion Dexius left in command. It was our third winter in the wilds, and we were sick of snow and hill mists, and the painted devils sniping at us from behind every gorse-bush; and we wanted to be able to drink with our friends in a wine shop, and walk twenty paces without wondering what was coming up behind us. And we cursed the Legate for being comfortable in Corstopitum, and grew to hate the sight of each other's faces.

I began to smell trouble coming, sure as acorns grow on oak trees.

And then one day when we had almost won through to spring, some of the men broke into the wine store and were found drunk on watch. They were put under guard, ready to be brought up before the Senior Centurion next day. And everyone knew what that meant. – He'd have been within his rights to order the death penalty; but being Daddy Dexius, who could be relied on to

be soft in such matters, they would probably get off with a flogging. Even so, it would be the kind of flogging that spreads a man flat on his face in the sick block for three days afterwards.

All the rest of that day you could feel the trouble like nearing thunder prickling in the back of your neck. And in the middle of supper, it came. Being the Eagle bearer, I ate in the Centurions' mess-hall, though in the lowest place there, next to the door; and I hadn't long sat down when the noise began.

It wasn't particularly loud, but there was an ugly note to it; a snarling note; and in the midst of it someone shouting, 'Come on, lads, let's get the prisoners out!' and other voices taking up the cry.

I remember Dexius's face as he got up and strode past me to the door; and suddenly knowing that we had all been quite wrong about him; that he wasn't soft at all. – More the kind of man who gets a reputation for being good-tempered and fair-game, because he knows that if he once lets his temper go and hits somebody he probably won't leave off till he's killed them.

I had only just started my supper, so I snatched a hard-boiled duck's egg from a bowl on the table and shoved it down the front of my uniform, and dashed out with the rest.

Outside on the parade-ground a crowd was gathering. Some of them had makeshift torches. The flare of them was teased by the thin wind that was blowing, and their light fell ragged on faces that were sullen and dangerous. Vipsanius the duty centurion was trying to deal with the situation, but he didn't seem to be having much success, and the crowd was getting bigger every moment.

Daddy Dexius said coolly, 'What goes on here, Centurion?'

'They're refusing to go on watch, Sir,' said Vipsanius. I mind he was sweating up a bit, despite the edge to the wind.

'We've had enough of going on watch in this dog-hole, night after filthy night!' someone shouted.

And his mates backed him up. 'How much longer are we going to squat here, making a free target of ourselves for the blue painted barbarians?'

'If Agricola wants to fight them, why

doesn't he come up and get things going?'

'Otherwise why don't we get out of here and go back where we came from?'

Men began shouting from all over the crowd, bringing up all the old soldiers' grievances about pay and leave and living conditions. 'We've had enough!' they shouted, 'We've had enough!'

'You'll have had more than enough, and the Painted People down on us, if you don't break up and get back on duty!' Vipsanius yelled back at them.

But the sullen crowd showed no sign of breaking up or getting back on duty. And suddenly, only half-believing, I understood just how ugly things might be going to turn. Not much harm done up to now, but if something, anything, tipped matters even a little in the wrong direction, the whole crowd could flare up into revolt, and revolt has a way of spreading that puts a heath-fire to shame.

Centurion Dexius said, 'Thank you, Centurion, I will take over now.' And then he glanced round for me. 'Standard-bearer.'

‘Here, Sir,’ says I, advancing smartly.

‘Go and fetch out the Eagle, and we’ll see if that will bring them to their senses.’

I left him standing there, not trying to shout them down or anything, just standing there, and went to fetch the Eagle.

In the Saccellum, part office and part treasury and part shrine, the lamp was burning on the table where the duty centurion would sit all night with his drawn sword before him – when not doing Rounds or out trying to quell a riot – and the Eagle on its tall shaft stood against the wall, with the Cohort standards ranged on either side of it.

I took it down; and as I did so its upward shadow, cast by the lamp on the table engulfed half the chamber behind it, as though some vast dark bird had spread wing and come swooping forward out of the gloom among the rafters. Used though I was to the Eagle standard, that great swoop of dark wings made me jump half out of my skin. But it was not the moment to be having fancies. I hitched up the Eagle into Parade Position, and out I went with it.

The Senior Centurion had quieted them down a bit; well, the look on his face would have quieted all Rome on a feast day; and when they saw the Eagle, their growling and muttering died away till I could hear a fox barking, way up the glen, and the vixen's scream in answer. But they still stood their ground, and I knew the quiet wouldn't last. And there was I, standing up with the Eagle, not knowing quite what to do next; and truth to tell, beginning to feel a bit of a fool. And then suddenly it came to me; what I had to do next; and I pulled out the duck's egg from inside my tunic and held it up.

And, 'Now look what you've done, you lot!' said I, 'Behaving like this you've upset the Eagle so much its laid an egg!'

I have noticed more than once in the years since then, that it is sometimes easier to swing the mood of a whole crowd than it is to swing the mood of one man on his own. Aye, a dicey thing is a crowd.

There was a moment of stunned silence, and then someone laughed, and someone else took up the laugh, and then more and more, a roar of laughter and a surge of stamping and back-slapping that swept away all that had gone before.

5

The Last Battle

And so we were still in Inchtuthil, and more or less in one piece, when the Legate came back to us, fat and prosperous as a moneylender after his winter in Corstopitum. And then Agricola came up from the Naval Base with the rest of the army, and as soon as the grass stood high enough to feed the cavalry horses, the advance was on again.

It was not easy going. No set-piece battles, but we had to fight for every hill pass and river ford; arrows came at us from every thicket, and once, the Painted Men fired the forest ahead of us when the wind was blowing our way. But at last, a weary long while it seemed since we marched from Inchtuthil, we came up towards the first dark wave-lift of the Grampians. – They call the place Mons Graupius, now; it hadn't got a

name then; at least it hadn't got a name in our tongue, it just seemed like the world's end. – And we had word back from the scouts that we had sent way up ahead, that Calgacus was waiting for us among the wooded gullies of the lower slopes, the whole Caledonian war-host with him.

Agricola halted the Legions, and gave orders for the usual war camp to be pitched.

The great square was measured out, and the banks and stockades thrown up; the General's pavilion set up in the midst of all, with the tents of the Legates on either side, and the Eagles of the four Legions ranged in front. The camp fires, one to each fifty men, were built in long straight rows, and the horse-lines and baggage park pegged out in position; the guards were posted and a meal of hard bannock and sour wine issued to all of us, and we settled in for the night.

But the nights are short in the north at that time of year, and it was morning soon enough, and Caledonians and Romans alike stirring for battle.

Tacitus, Agricola's son-in-law, who

wrote a history of that campaign later, sets down a fine fiery dawn-of-battle speech for Calgacus. I learned it almost by heart, in after years, for it's a good speech though not over polite to us Romans.

Something like this, it went: 'My brothers, – this I bid you to remember when the war horns sound: There is nothing beyond us but the sea; and even on the sea the galleys of the Red Crests prowl like wolf packs. Therefore there can be no retreat for us, we conquer or we die. And we shall conquer! The Roman victories came not by their strength but by our weakness, and our weakness was that we were many Tribes divided among ourselves. Now we stand together as one People, and we are strong! They are fewer in number than we, they are strangers under strange skies; the mountains and the forests are enemies to them and friends to us. . . . My brothers, we have this choice: victory at whatever cost, and freedom, or the Roman yoke upon our necks, our women enslaved, our young men carried off to serve the Romans at the other end of the world! We have heard of the Roman Peace, but in truth, they make a desolation and call it Peace! Keep that in your hearts as you rush into battle!'

Aye, a good rabble-rousing speech. – Though come to think of it, I wonder how Tacitus knew what he said, or if he said anything like that at all.

I do know what Agricola said, for I heard him, when he harangued us, standing on a tub of arrowheads.

'Comrades,' says he, 'we have fought through more than one campaign together. I think that you have been content with your General; I know that I have been well enough satisfied with my soldiers.' (I thought about the Eagle and the egg!) 'We have pushed on further than all other of our armies, and here we stand in the farthest part of Britain, where never any man carried the Eagles before. But though the land is strange to us, the men we fight today are the same as those we fought and routed and forced back in earlier time. They ran then, and they'll run again; it is because they are so good at running that they have lasted so long. So now, lads – one

good sharp heave for the glory of old Mother Rome, and the thing is done!'

And we cheered him until our cheering echoed back from the dark woods and the mountain corries.

Well then, our battle line was drawn up, the lightly armed foot-soldiers of the auxiliary cohorts in the centre, the cavalry on the wings, and the heavy troops of the Legions drawn up behind, along the line of last night's banks and ditches. The Ninth was held in reserve, and we didn't think much of that, but it's a job somebody has to do.

That was my first full-pitched battle, and I'll not be forgetting it in a hurry. I'll not be forgetting the great wave of the Caledonian chariot charge thundering down upon our battle line; and the way our line swayed and bulged a bit, but held firm, and the charge broke, like a wave breaking on rocks, and curled back on itself. Our lads charged forward after them; and it was then that Calgacus sent in a second charge, sweeping down from the hills and circling wide to take our battle-mass from the rear. It was red and ancient

chaos after that, though the cavalry did their job finely, and the banks and ditches of the camp itself played a useful part in throwing the Caledonian chariots into confusion. Aye, a bad patch, and they all but crumpled up our left wing, and for a while the battle could have gone either way. It was six cohorts of the Ninth, pushed up from the reserve to thicken the battle line, that saved the situation and held it, steady as a rock, while the Fourteenth had a chance to re-form and rally to their own Eagle. The old Ninth has come on evil days since then, but I shan't forget that, either; the spread wings of our Eagle bright in sunlight, and the Roman battle-mass staggering and then growing steady again, and thrusting forward. . . .

The fighting began a little after sun-up; and before the sun stood at noon the Caledonian war-host was a broken rabble, being hunted through their forests and across their heather moors by us victorious Romans. At nightfall the hunt was called off, for it is not good to hunt even a broken enemy through strange country in the dark. And when

the moon rose, it shone down – have you ever noticed how coldly uncaring the moon can seem? – on smashed chariots and dead horses, and dead men among the blood-sodden heather.

That was when I saw Calgacus; the only time. I saw him by the cold moonlight, lying at the foot of the slope where the fighting had been heaviest, with the finest of his warriors about him, and his long hair tangled into the roots of a pale flowered bramble bush.

Our losses were officially put at three hundred and sixty, including Valarius, a Centurion of the Ninth, and one young fool of a Tribune who rode right into a rear-guard fight at the edge of the woods. The Caledonians lost thousands; more than half their war-host, besides those that were taken captive.

Calgacus had staked everything, the whole fighting strength of Caledonia, on that last battle; and when it was over the war in Caledonia was over too.

Three days later the Senior Centurion sent for me to his tent. He was rubbing his chin with a piece of pumice when I went in. – He was one of the few soldiers

I have known who always contrived to keep a smooth chin even on campaign. – And he laid down the pumice and felt his jaw enquiringly for traces of a beard.

'I am promoting Centurion Gaurus to Centurion Valarius's place. You will take over Gaurus's century,' he said. Just like that!

'Sir,' I said. I felt a bit winded. And yet truth to tell, I wasn't altogether surprised. Somebody was due for promotion, with Valarius having got himself killed, and I knew I'd done well in the battle. I suppose I puffed my chest out a bit.

And suddenly he laughed, 'And you can take that smirk off your face. You carried out your duties extremely well when the Painted Men nearly crumpled up our left wing; in fact one might say with courage and devotion; but Roma Dea! What else do you think the Legions expect of their standard-bearers? That business about the Eagle and the egg, now, I'm not at all sure it wasn't disrespect to the gods, but it ended a very nasty situation, and showed that you have the trick of handling men. Go and take over from Gaurus. – Oh, wait—' and he picked up a roughly trimmed hazel stick, – we'd hacked down a bit of hazel and thorn scrub when we were clearing the ground for the camp – and tossed it to me. 'This will serve you for your vine-staff until we get back to Eburacum and it can be changed for the proper thing. Your promotion will have to be confirmed then, too, but I think you need not worry about that. Lucius will take over from you as Eagle-bearer.'

And he picked up his bit of pumice again and got back to work on his chin.

6

Return to Eburacum

It was late into the autumn when the Ninth came marching back into Eburacum, and the crowds gathered to watch us in as they had gathered to watch us march out, more than three years ago; but I could see no sign of Cordaella among them. Not that you can look about you overmuch when you're on the march. I told myself that was why I had missed her, and there was no need to be anxious. But of course I was anxious all the same; and the first instant that I could get town leave, I was off to look for her.

But passing the Camp Commandant's house on the way to the Main Gate, I was pulled up short by a familiar sound; the small sharp 'Tip-tip-tap' of a light hammer and chisel cutting the tiny squares for a picture-floor. I knew that sound too well to be mistaken in it. At any rate Vedrix had not gone back to Lindum.

I doubled round a corner and through a side door, following my ears, as you might say, and across a small courtyard beyond, and finally ran Vedrix himself to ground, squatting amid his little cubes of chalk and sandstone and brick and shale, in what looked like a new bath-house sticking out from the Camp Commandant's quarters.

He looked up, grinning that foxy grin of his, when I appeared.

'Good morning to you, Centurion.'

'You know then,' I said, stopping in my tracks.

'One hears these things.'

I sketched him a kind of mock salute. 'Centurion, Sixth Century, Ninth Cohort. That's about the lowest form of life in the Centurions' Mess.' And then my anxiety caught up with me, and I burst out in a rush, 'But it does mean that I can marry now, if – if –' and I couldn't bring out the last bit at all.

'If Cordaella hasn't changed her mind?' said Vedrix.

'How is it with Cordaella? Three years is a long time.'

'It was all well with her less than an hour ago. But three years is a long time, even as you say; and maybe you had best go and ask her herself, before it gets any longer.'

'I'll be doing that!' I said, and departed without waiting to take my leave.

I had to pass quite close to the well where I had first spoken to her, to reach her house; but I think I would have gone that way even if it had been a round about journey. I had a feeling. . . .

And there she was, her red hair lighting up the grey little street, just as I remembered. She had filled the pail and set it on the well curb beside her. And she was just sitting there, half-turned to gaze down into the water. She looked somehow as though she had been sitting there quite a while.

But she did not look up when I came along the street; not till I was standing right beside her.

'That pail is much too heavy for a little bird like you,' I said, 'Let me carry it home for you.'

She looked up then, as I reached for the pail; and next instant it wasn't the pail that I had hold of, it was Cordaella, and she had her arms round my neck and was half laughing and half crying and clinging on to me as though she never meant to let go. And I – well I won't say I wasn't doing my share of the hugging, too.

'I didn't see you when we marched in yesterday,' I said 'Why did you not come out with everybody else to see us marching back?'

'I was so afraid,' she said.

'Afraid?'

She nodded against my shoulder. 'That when the Eagle came up the street, I would not see you there.'

'Well I'd not have been carrying the Eagle, but you would have seen me at the head of my Cohort,' I said, 'Cordaella, I have my vine staff now.'

'I know,' she said. 'We heard later. Quintus, I am so proud of you!'

I wanted to boast a bit, seem big in her eyes; but I've never been a very good liar. 'I didn't get it for being a hero,' I told her. 'I got it for making a bad joke at the right moment.'

'We heard about that, too,' she said, soft with laughter. And then she suddenly turned grave, and held me off at arms' length, and stood looking at me. 'I do not believe that your great strong Roman Legions that march about in straight lines and build square forts would ever choose their Centurions just for making jokes at the right moment,' she said. 'But anyhow, I am thinking that people who make bad jokes at the right moment are maybe much easier to be married to, than heroes.'

Within a year, Agricola had been recalled to Rome, and the whole Fourteenth Legion had been pulled out from Britain to strengthen the German Frontier. That mean that Inchtuthil and all the Northern forts had to be abandoned; and almost the whole campaign was wasted. But that's the way it is with armies on the frontiers and governments at home. . . .

Well, there you are. At any rate it got me my first Century, and you younglings a British grandmother.

Throw another log on the fire.

More Beaver Books

We hope you have enjoyed this Beaver Book. Here are some of the other titles:

A Circlet of Oak Leaves An exciting story of heroism and courage set in second-century Roman Britain specially written for younger readers by Rosemary Sutcliff, with vivid illustrations by Victor Ambrus

The Four Grannies Erg and Emily have no fewer than four grannies between them, and when their parents go away and all four decide to help at once, trouble is bound to start. . . . A very funny story for younger readers by Diana Wynne Jones; illustrated by Thelma Lambert

Crockle Adrift When Crockle takes a fancy to Mrs Noah's new sunhat he falls overboard and has to be rescued by Jaffet and Jannet – and the hat becomes surprisingly useful! Written and drawn by John Ryan for younger readers

These and many other Beavers are available from your local bookshop or newsagent, or can be ordered direct from: Hamlyn Paperback Cash Sales, PO Box 11, Falmouth, Cornwall TR10 9EN. Send a cheque or postal order made payable to the Hamlyn Publishing Group, for the price of the book plus postage at the following rates:
UK: 40p for the first book, 18p for the second book, and 13p for each additional book ordered to a maximum charge of £1.49;
BFPO and Eire: 40p for the first book, 18p for the second book, plus 13p per copy for the next 7 books and thereafter 7p per book;
OVERSEAS: 60p for the first book and 18p for each extra book.

New Beavers are published every month and if you would like the *Beaver Bulletin*, a newsletter which tells you about new books and gives a complete list of titles and prices, send a large stamped addressed envelope to:

Beaver Bulletin
The Hamlyn Group
Astronaut House
Feltham
Middlesex TW14 9AR

204715